View from the Mountaintop
A Journey Into Wholeness

A Contemplative, Inspirational
Book of Poems

Lee Ann Fagan Dzelzkalns

AGELESS DOMINION PUBLISHING
P.O. BOX 11546
MILWAUKEE, WI 53211

Ageless Dominion Publishing
P.O. Box 11546
Milwaukee, WI 53211

Edited by Rhonda L. Foster
Illustrations and Desktop Publishing by Cathryn L. Denny
Back Cover Photo by Diane Yokes

First Printing: November 1995

Library of Congress Catalog Card Number: 95-80180

ISBN 1-881300-01-3

Printed in the United States of America

To the loving memory of my mother, who,
after her transition, taught me how to soar
from the mountain's top

To my sons, Justin and Ryan, may you
continue to expand your consciousness,
learning life's lessons, and allow the wings
of grace to gently guide you on your path

To those of you unaware of the Essence
of Spirit, yet

To those of you contemplating the path

To those of you walking the path

To those of you who have become the path

. . . the view from the mountaintop is yours

Ageless Dominion Publishing

It is our mission to offer works that contribute to the expansion of the self, the realization of wholeness and the connectedness of it ALL. Thus, we recognize that in healing and expanding individually, we impact collectively and globally the well-being of our planet.

Rhonda L. Foster, Editor

Rhonda is as light as her heart, helping people along their paths. With a bachelor's degree in journalism and experience editing emergency medicine and holistic health publications, Rhonda offers creative expression from her soul. An artist by nature, her talents are many. Currently, she is a massage therapist, working with psychologists and physical therapists to combine the power of touch with the power of the mind. Her diverse nature offers itself fully to embrace the intention of this author's work.

Cathryn L. Denny, Illustrator

As a young girl, Cathy was encouraged by a supportive family to explore and discover her artist gifts. With a degree in Visual Communications, Cathy has a flourishing business, Denny Design, in Milwaukee, Wisc., that encompasses all aspects of illustrating and desktop publishing. A truly inspired artist, Cathy sincerely connects with clarity to produce illuminating works of art. This book reveals the inner wisdom guiding her hand.

Contents

Acknowledgments IX

Preface XI

The Source of All Being XV

Daily Prayers:
- Prayer of Service..XVI
- A Nighttime Wish XVI
- Prayer of Protection XVII
- Thankfulness XVIII
- Group Invocation for Wholeness XIX

Introduction: The Nature of Being Whole® 1

Gateway I: Decondition the Self

Release to See 7

Time to Fly 11

Lessons 12

Acceptance 15

Echo of Love 19

Letting Go 20

Be Still 21

Detachment 23

Conditioned Thoughts 27

Synchronicity.. 28

The Self 29

Mirror Reflection... 30

Purpose 32

Gateway II: Recondition the Self

Renew to Thee.. 37

Reality or Illusion? 39

Objective Reality 40
Truth 42
The Simple 43
Light 44
Listen 45
Clarity 48
Forgiveness 50
Angel Wings 52
Surrender...55
Lightheartedness 56
Inner Guidance 58
Inner Life...59
Be and Receive 61
Balance 62
It Is What it Is 63
Honor..64

Gateway III: The Unconditioned Self

Come to Be 69
Transformation 71
To Be.. 73
Awareness Rising 75
Unfoldment 77
I Miss You 79
Compassionate Detachment 80
Suspend Yourself and Relax 81
Communion With Thee 82
I Am 85
The Essence of Spirit 86
Feel the Flow of Spirit 88
Pure Love 90
The Moon 92
Believe Me When I Say I Am 93
The Nature of God 95

Afterword... 97
Key Concepts 99
Guided Meditation 105

Acknowledgments

My heart is filled with loving gratitude to the Essence of ALL that IS (God). The lessons I have learned thus far have transmuted my entire nature of being. I am tremendously thankful for all the inspired teachers that have presented themselves to me. As we learn from others, we teach, and as we teach, we learn from others. Christine, I still hear you ... thank you for your continued support.

I would like to thank Rhonda, my editor, for her limitless devotion in maintaining the integrity of this work. Her depth of understanding and spiritual nature allowed the compilation of this work to flow harmoniously.

To my illustrator and long-time friend, Cathy, I thank you. Your essence graces these pages with eloquence and perfection.

For the past several years I have been blessed with the emergence of my soul family (individuals with which I have a deep sense of knowingness). To my reviewers and dear friends, Susan Ann Niederlander, JoAnn Fabritz, Monica Allen, and Kunter Akay, your unconditional giving was a gift I shall always remember. My gratitude is beyond words for all we have shared together. This expression from my heart also reaches out to Cam, Vick, Diana, Dave, Chris, Jodie, Mike, Diane, Pat, JoAnn L., Barb, Annie, Jill, Rosie and Mary. Yes!

To my grandmother Sally Dziedzic, who instilled in me the strength of character, the expansiveness of my heart, and the fullness of my soul. Thank you, grandma, for feeding me words of wisdom when I was young; it all came back to me when I needed it most.

To my father and to my brother, David, thank you for widening your vision to take in the limitless possibilities surrounding each of you.

A special note of thanks to my Monday group (Josh, Cheryl, Kunter, Gail, Gwen, Pam, Christine, Brian, Laurie, Rhonda, Diane, Jodie, …) for all the lessons we have learned together, the sharing, tears, moments of silence, emerging into Oneness, … group work is powerful work.

To my students and clients past and present.
Thank you for your courage and ability to stretch yourselves and believe in your full potential.

To Nicole, for your awesome dedication to my family.
Your assistance at home has given me the opportunity to do all that I am to do for the greater good of all concerned.

A special thank-you to my in-laws, Dzidra and Roberts, for your unconditional nature and for being on call 24 hours a day.

A big hug to my friends in the community of Whitefish Bay, and to Terri, thanks for understanding the nature of my work.

Justin and Ryan, my sons, I thank you for respecting my quiet time in the cloud room as inspiration moved me. Our love is etched in the realm of divineness. We shall continue to evolve in this love, truth and wisdom of the new age.

To Ray, my husband, my partner, my friend.
You have expanded my vision through the expression of being who you are each day. You are my greatest teacher. Thank you for believing in me unconditionally, even when you saw me repeating another life lesson. Your patience, compassion and pure love guided me through times of darkness and despair.
I love you.

And thanks to all of you who have touched my life by merely passing by me on the street with a smile in your heart and love in your soul. We are all connected in the Great Sea of Oneness, and I continue to be grateful for the abundance that is all ours.

Preface

"Belief is the key that opens the gateway door.
Truth of the Divine Spark within expands
consciousness to soar."
— Lee Ann Fagan Dzelzkalns

I was nudged out of bed at 2:00 a.m. by a deep sense of knowing. An inspiration and flow of words streamed through my consciousness as my hand wrote voraciously to keep up. Shortly after, it dawned on me that I had prayed a week prior for my love of creating poetry to reveal itself again. I wanted so much to write as I did when I was a young girl. This time, however, the verses are filled with clarity and purpose.

For months, I continued to express from my essence words that lovingly guided and directed my life's intention. The entire concept of wholeness coupled with the symbology of the triangle kept echoing in my altered state. Each individual poem seemed to place itself in an order of rightness. This natural order then manifested into gateways of self-awareness, self-expansion and self-realization. It became more clear that the nature of being whole is my understanding of harmonizing and synthesizing the physical, mental, emotional, and spiritual self (the body, heart and soul), which leads to a greater sense of knowledge and wisdom.

This book of poems is an esoteric interpretation of my journey toward wholeness. These words represent a sharing of life's lessons. Although our lessons are individual in nature, we can all learn from one another's experience. These thoughts and insights serve as a guide. They explain how conditioned we are and what we need to do to expand our sense of self. These lessons of understanding, forgiving, releasing, accepting, knowing, trusting, and unconditionally loving provide a conduit for the integration of mind, body and spirit—our essence.

Your true essence (that is, your true state of being, the individual connected to the ultimate divine nature of the Self, as opposed to existence itself) has always been whole. Yet somehow, you, like so many others, have drifted apart from knowing your goodness and greatness in wholeness. Now is the time to embrace your essence and expand your concept of self.

The head (ego) can keep you very busy in the external world of form (i.e. doing this, doing that, running as fast as you can on the treadmill of life). The dis-ease (as opposed to disease) of encumbered living produces traumatic overtures on your sense of well-being. It can keep you far, far away from the inner reality of your true essence. When the ego is fragmented, the physical body is not happy, the mental body is caught in negative cycles, and the emotional body is on the "poor me" path. The ego maintains a grip on the past by replaying old scripts (i.e. thoughts of failure or feelings of inadequacy) and firmly spearheads the emotionalizing of the self. Until you make a choice to break the cycle of fear or anger or resentment, self-doubt, self-rejection, etc., you will be caught in its continuous cycle. Know that it is within yourself to harmonize and synthesize the physical, mental and emotional self, which will provide a healthy, balanced and whole personality. Now is the time to open to a shift in consciousness. The ego does not have to be in control. You can learn to recognize the activity of the heart and intuitively follow its signals.

A gateway symbolizes moving from what was in the past, to the truth of what is in that moment. Soar beyond the known into the crispness of new beginnings and create an opportunity to explore, emerge and expand. Flow and blend with all aspects of your beingness emotionally, mentally, physically and spiritually.

Through contemplation you will make choices and pass through gateways of understanding that gently and mystically guide you toward wholeness. Your individual path embodies a vibration that guides you from the core of your individuality. And yet, as you venture forward in faith and truth, you will revel in the knowledge that what you have been striving to achieve within yourself has always been by nature who you are. You will learn, as I have, that when you release the need to be someone, you come to realize that you have always been that someone.

As you become fully conscious of ALL that you are, you can allow the infinite creative potential to reach the heavens from your depths, for the heavens lie within. As you take this perspective of wholeness and voyage inside to your cellular being and acknowledge all your goodness, all your worth, all your strength and peace … you make yourself available to commune with the Essence of ALL and ignite your inner flame in rightness and truth. (This Essence, with a capital E, is the ultimate divine nature of the Infinite Self, the Oneness of Source and illumined within us.)

This is a journey of life, your personal journey. The poems will guide you along in what may feel like a flowing, synchronous, eternal moment. You may find the words gripping you when you least expect it. You may feel the pages hugging you when you need a hug. You may sense the gentleness of the rhythm and rhyme comforting you as if lulled in a rocking chair. You may experience a rush or release of blocked energy leaving your body. You may willingly receive a gush of love pouring off the page into your heart. You may encounter an overwhelming sense of self-acceptance and unconditional love. You may experience an instantaneous healing … just let it happen. Let yourself be with the words, the verse, the essence of it all.

I know there is great truth to what is presented to you between the covers of this book. The gifts you may receive will be unique and individual to you. I encourage you to remain open and willing to the unlimited possibilities within.

Now, I recommend prior to reading "View from the Mountaintop: A Journey Into Wholeness," that you sit quietly, get silent and comfortable. Then turn to a desired poem or allow your fingers to be guided to the poem that is meant for you in that moment. Release yourself in the dance of the inner rhythm vibrating amidst the boundless, infinite universal realm of ALL and take in the view of the mountaintop. Through your own self-exploration and self-discovery, you will experience the essence of being whole.

Love to you all.

In truth & wholeness,

Lee Ann Fagan Dzelzkalns

Lee Ann Fagan Dzelzkalns

The Source of All Being

How we individually label and call upon the Source of our existence is a private and personal expression. To maintain a sense of universality within this book, I use several names for "The Source," such as Essence, God, and Truth. I encourage you to replace my terms with what feels good to you.

You may also try to work through the uncomfortableness, trusting in what feels right. Get with someone to share and discuss what is being impressed upon you. You may discover, as I have, that although we practice diverse beliefs, religions and rituals, the underlying foundation for all is unconditional love. And, this unconditional love is what we all connect to our individual "Source." The words may be different as we pray, but a common ground is shared in our belief in the interconnectedness of life. McLaughlin and Davidson demonstrate this best in their book "Spiritual Politics":

"The Kingdom of God is within you" (Christian—Jesus)

"Look within, thou art the Buddha" (Buddhism—Buddha)

"By understanding the Self all this universe is known" (Hindu—The Upanishads)

"He who knows himself knows his Lord" (Moslem—Muhammad)

"Man, know thyself and thou shalt know the universe and the gods" (Ancient Greek)

Thank you for your anticipated openness and willingness to lovingly read these words from your heart, through your eyes, with your soul.

Daily Prayers

These prayers are an offering of love. They are yours to receive and embrace. Use them in conjunction with the book or offer them up on their own. You may say them in directed consciousness, clearly visualizing the process, or simply be with the essence of your intention. Allow yourself space to get centered (settle your entire being) and be with the verse and your inner guidance.

Prayer of Service

I am flowing love, light and presence,
As I blend with the highest of Essence.
I am open and available in this day,
To God's Grace and unfolding way.

A Nighttime Wish

As I wish upon this star
My intention travels, jettisoning far.
Lifting to the Essence known,
The realm of guidance I am shown.

Prayer of Protection

I pray for protection in the name of universal
peace and love
And in the light of the omniscient Oneness
within and above.
This power is stronger than any power
known in heaven and earth,
Gently guiding my hand from the beginning
of time, my birth.

I pray for the protection of my aura
sealed in a cone of light,
Laced in the brilliance of gold and white,
a mirror reflection so bright.
Anything of the false nature bounces off
this suit with care,
Sending back to the source rightness
from the Essence we share.

I thank you, Universal Essence/God,
for your loving protection this day.
As I continue to serve from my heart,
the Love, the Light, and the Way.

Thankfulness

I am thankful for the Presence of Spirit
unconditionally guiding my hand.
I am thankful for the Presence of Spirit
as I feel my heart lovingly expand.

I am thankful for the Presence of Spirit
filling my breath with strength.
I am thankful for the Presence of Spirit,
patience growing in length.

I am thankful for the Presence of Spirit
expressing Truth through me.
I am thankful that I have awakened
to reclaim my essence "to be."

I am thankful for the Presence of Spirit
enlightening my vision to see.
I am thankful for the Presence of Spirit
illuminating my soul through thee.

I am thankful for the abundance
that is truly mine this day.
I am thankful for the Essence of ALL,
it IS the way of the Way.

Group Invocation for Wholeness

As we lovingly invoke the Hierarchy of Divine Mastery,
we humbly give thanks for this shared consciousness.

May we always be aware as we awaken to our realization,
our connectedness to Source and the Kingdom within.

May our minds be open to the Divine illumination of Truth.

May our hearts reveal their essence of unconditional love.

May our bodies be a harmonious, disciplined home for our souls.

May our souls be infused with a balanced self.

May our intuitive eye clearly see our life's purpose.

May our words communicate with clarity and compassion.

May our eyes bless all that we behold.

May our energy be in atonement with Infinite Source/
Essence/God.

May the nature of wholeness and unconditional love be
awakened in the heart and soul of the Planet.

We lovingly allow these qualities to stream forth to nourish
and illumine the Universal consciousness in humankind.

Yes!

Journey of the self
toward the Self

Introduction

The Nature of Being Whole®

You are reading this book for a higher reason
than you may consciously know. As you develop
your awareness and knowledge about your
entire sense of being, you will understand more and
more. Your thirst will become voracious as you seek and
find answers to questions, solutions to problems, and
truths revealed. It's all about acknowledging your
higher self, your intuitive self, the will of your soul.
(We're really just one great pool of energetic souls
waiting to serve the world.) When we open to our
essence, the Essence of ALL that IS can then filter its
Great Love through us so we may serve in all areas of
our lives, from play to work. In this service, we discover
the sweet scent of life filled with unconditional love and
wisdom of the ages.

The poetic words within may gently guide you through
the veils of illusion that challenge your physical, mental
and emotional well-being. You may break through the
obstacles and patterns of conditioned programming
such as the need to always be in control, the inability to
receive gifts or compliments from others, the refusal to
nurture yourself while caring for others, the feelings of
inadequacy or not being good enough, the fear of failure,
the inability to trust, the inability to share, the need to
guard the heart from the pain of the past, and so forth.
Conscious awareness will expand your vision to see and
acknowledge the fear of the past. Once you recognize the
patterns and have the willingness to break them, you are
on your way to embracing all your goodness in Godness.

The spirit of your creative essence will reveal itself as you open to your true nature. Just as the goat climbs the mountain and transcends its egoic self into the nature of the unicorn—its true self—you, too, can emerge into one whole. The separate parts will no longer exist. As you begin the climb to the mountaintop, you move toward balance and unification of the ego/head and the essence/heart.

I have categorized three gateways to assist you in moving along the pathway and reaching the mountaintop. Remember, these gateways are mere symbols to your own personal growth and spiritual expansion. It is up to you to reach inside, dig deep, and seek the truth within. The skills of relaxation, meditation, and contemplation can greatly assist you in self-discovery and expression. For this purpose, a guided meditation is presented on page 105.

Gateway I guides you into the process of purging, releasing, renewing and releasing. Surprisingly, you will discover how wonderful it is to completely get in touch with the anxiety and fear that has been embedded in the depths of your cellular memory. Self-exploration will open you to the known in the unknown, as you trust in that knowing. This gateway leads through the **deconditioning** of the self. Here, you experience a release of the conditioned habits into a creative consciousness of goodness and unconditional love steeped in a higher sense of awareness. This is a continual process of change and growth. The rendition of this cycle is a psychospiritual rhythm set by your willingness to evolve in your heart, mind and soul. Recognize that the cycle will repeat itself when it serves your highest good to advance up the mountain.

Gateway II begins reconditioning the self in a gentle shift of understanding. A positive perspective replaces what was once a negative downward spiral. Here, your conditioned self learns how to break barriers and decondition from old ways to create a new threshold of living. Your **reconditioned** self will embrace the straight and narrow path and seek answers to all questions and contemplative moments. Seek and ye shall find ... if you don't ask, how will you ever know? If you don't knock on the door, how can it ever be opened? You will see your entire sense of being, physically, mentally and emotionally, so you can bring balance, harmony and synthesis to all aspects of yourself.

Gateway III illumines the self, the **unconditioned** self. Think about the possibilities of the unconditioned self. You are free to be all that you are within the realm of all unlimited possibilities, free to be your essence connected to the Essence of ALL that IS. Yes! To be! You begin to experience the embrace of the Oneness in your heart, mind, body and soul. The light of your soul finds its purpose. It finds its connection within your heart. Here you approach the top of the mountain and literally feel the emergence of the soul infusing with the body, mind and emotions. This is where life is lived fully. This is where life is lived wholly. This is the essence of being whole.

As you read this book, imagine yourself somewhere on the mountain trail. Lovingly flow with this image and trust in the process. In this image, allow yourself to be free of judgment as you page through this book. Read the verses and then ponder over them. What do they mean to you? Contemplate. Just be with them and sit in silence. Allow your inner guidance, your higher self, to provide you space to learn with discernment and loving detachment. Just be in the eternal present moment and express your connectedness to it ALL.

Gateway 1

Decondition the Self

Release to See

"The forest will answer you
in the way you call to it."
— Finnish Proverb

To decondition the self is to release yourself from the confines of past judgment and emotional attachment. An awareness and clearing of subconscious cultural and societal programming takes place. The judgments of personal perceptions and interpretations lose their influence as you begin to express what is in true affirmation in your life. As you consciously decondition, you can reject the error of false thought, negative thinking or any idea of lack in your life. Instead, you will own right thinking and the power of knowing your own heart. Through this, you create the ability to discover all that you truly are.

Insights and illuminations will present themselves to you as you awaken your conscious awareness. Effort and commitment to break cycles, move through conditioned patterns, release association of thought, and empty out is a ritual in self-awareness and renewal. Your personal mantra may go from "I know I can, I know I can," to "I am all that I am, I am all that I AM."

Moving through a gateway may be painful at times, but it is part of the learning. Your body will let you know if you haven't dealt with an issue or problem. The emotion will embed further into your cellular

> ## Decondition the self from—
>
> - Material glamour
>
> - The seduction of the world of senses
>
> - Perceived needs that cultivate the ego's perception that "I am someone important"
>
> - The world of duality and the ego separated from your inner world
>
> - Negative emotions of separation such as fear, anger, and loneliness
>
> - Self-imposed limitations
>
> - The debilitating programming of past perceptions

memory, building a solid, thick wall of protection. If you notice tightness in your solar plexus, reflect on the immediate situation that stimulated your physiology. The lessons may become more clear. A guarded heart is a major battle to overcome. You may discover your own shielded heart when you begin taking responsibility for your feelings and enforcing self-awareness strategies. When you recognize your patterns of behavior, you can begin to release and break them. As you become aware and accepting of what is, you then can move on to the next unfolding level of self-expansion.

Awaiting you on the other side of the gate is the breath of new beginnings and insights. The duality of my lessons has taught me that peace and happiness can be born from the wisdom in disharmony and sadness. As I become more in touch with my true sense of self, as each layer of conditional, emotional release reveals itself, I am all the more clear and free. When I was learning about detachment, for example, I came to realize my attachment to certain things and certain people. I found myself agonizing over how to get to that neutral space in between attachment and detachment. But, I also found that the power of letting go and trusting in the Essence of ALL that IS accelerated my process of growth and expansion. I trusted. I cultivated spiritual self-reliance by learning to listen and feel from my heart. When I embraced both ends of the spectrum (attachment and detachment), I comfortably met peace in the neutral space between the two.

To lovingly claim truth in your life, begin with owning your flaws and strengths. Balance of your physical, mental and emotional self is the first step toward synthesis of the whole self in soul and personality. The journey up the mountain is a climb. But, with each step, we grow closer to our peace of mind, desires of the heart, health of the body, and knowledge of the Absolute. With each breath, we renew ourselves into a realm of continual expansion and eternal knowingness, a knowingness that we are more than matter in this external world of form, we are spirit manifesting as divine matter.

self-awareness

Time to Fly

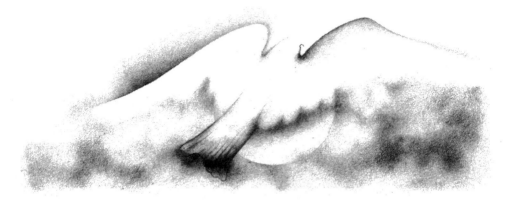

Wings spread open
It's time to fly.
Others will stop you
Or at least they will try.

Listen to your heart,
The answers are there.
Begin at the start,
Love unconditionally, always be fair.

It is in the moment,
As you will see,
That people will either hear you,
Be awakened, or flee.

Be true to yourself
In all that you do.
The Essence is Divine.
Now it is time to be you!

Lessons

You can go through life without a clue
of what it's all about.
Or take the time to go within,
unfolding a purposeful route.
Your mission on earth is unique
and special to only you,
It's about learning lessons,
inner strength, and being true.

Others may tell you what to do
as you journey down your path
Be open in your thought,
release insecurities or feelings of wrath.
Know that you have all the power
within to do great things.
The answers lie at your center,
dig deep, see what it brings.

How do you listen to
what life's lessons really teach?
Wait for unfoldment,
this will challenge you to reach.
Then the impression will come
about what you are to learn,
You will open your awareness
to tackle every turn.

The same lessons come back
      time again if you do not act,
This is more than observation,
      this is a universal fact.
When you get caught up
      in a pattern that won't let go,
Recognize what is happening,
      then move through it slow.

Realize that life is an educational tool
      striving to instruct.
The vision of what we create
      for ourselves isn't fate or luck.
What we do with the instruction
      and how we learn from it,
Is the difference between flowing
      in life or wanting to quit.

Life's lessons come in all disguises
      as you discover within,
To further your advancement here,
      stretching yourself to win.
It's not about winning a race,
      or being better than another,
It is inner love, integrity,
      and loving your sisters and brothers.

Know the choice is truly yours,
      the impression is in your heart,
You decide to learn or not,
      there is no trial to finish or start.
Your journey is an accumulation
      of everything up until now,
Respect yourself where you are
      on your path and lovingly allow.

Acceptance

When you step into this world you are filled
    with limitless potential,
You have not had much time to be cautioned
    about the influential.
But this limitless potential is within you
    for all your existence,
You just need to recognize your goodness
    with love and persistence.

The fact remains so clear to embrace
    all that you are,
Accept yourself for the essence in you,
    let go of contracted scars.
Limiting scars are mental thoughts
    produced only by you,
Acknowledge what they are, release them,
    - say they are through!

Try not to give them power, otherwise
    they will grow and grow,
Do you know what I mean?
    Have you ever made yourself feel low?
The choice is yours to peer deep
    within your heart,
Realize you are a wonderful being,
    every inner and outer part.

To accept yourself unconditionally means
there are no limitations.
To value yourself as a worthy human being,
an incredible creation.
It really doesn't matter
what other people think,
It is up to you what counts,
this is truly the missing link.

When you believe in yourself and the truth
of your being,
You will open your inner eyes to illumination,
clarity in seeing.
Trust as you go within yourself, flow
with unfoldment of grace,
This is your essence, your spiritual source
it will bring light to your face.

As you learn the acceptance of self,
you will live from the inside out.
This will make a difference in daily living,
you will see without a doubt.
If you want to change how you view yourself
strictly on the outside.
Think about your inner dialog
at the center of which you abide.

You are filled with inner integrity,
honor yourself through and through,
Make the day special, affirm your goodness,
embrace all that is new.
It is in your personal transformation
that growth continues to soar,
As you accept the goodness of Grace
bestowed upon you forevermore.

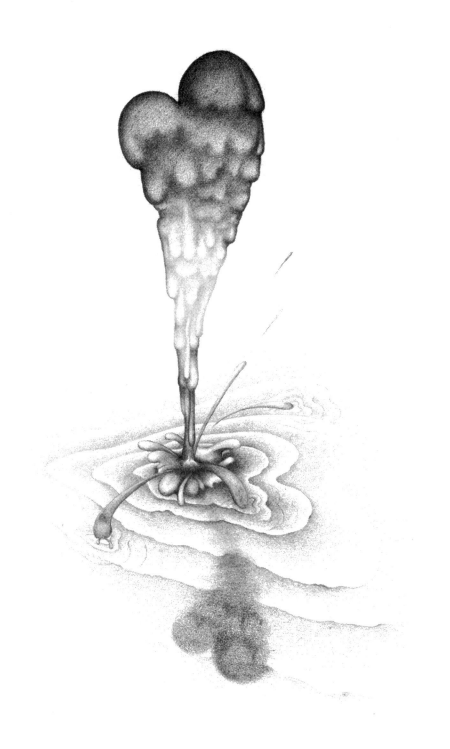

Echo of Love

The vibrational echo of love courses through
      all of me,
Tracing elements of tranquil living,
        pent-up discomfort set free.

Love lingers longingly through my essence,
       my savoring soul,
It awakens a yearning and a thirst,
        to release past perceptions and roles.

For the message of love is overwhelmingly pure,
        as it reflects the field of Grace.
Lifting and clarifying the mystical presence of
        white light enveloping Truth's face.

So I clear my thoughts of what it may be,
To embrace the moment's perfection of loving
       lightly all of thee.

To dismiss the definition of how others relate
       to love,
But to feel, taste, and recognize my heart's
       echo from the heavens above.

For the dimension of love is beyond all words,
       expressed in a humble surround.
The knowingness so deeply imbued to be lived
       and shared, a gift oh so profound.

The echo of love.

Letting Go

Your beingness is light and free,
No matter where you are.
Teach others now about "how to be"
They will awaken and reach far.

As you surrender and lift up high,
To a knowingness that is real.
Stretch yourself to the majestic sky,
As feet nestle in the earth to feel.

Rather than question your sense of direction,
Or why it is up to you.
Let yourself make the natural selection,
Truly let go and lovingly do.

Be Still

The moment of stillness is overwhelming
     as you embrace inner peace,
It takes you to a different dimension,
     very sovereign, provoking release.
To get quiet and go within yourself, to listen
     in this meditative state,
Is about expanding your awareness, walking
     through the spiritual gate.

As you become still in meditation,
     you will free your mind of thought,
You will detach from all impressions
     and associations you were taught.
Go ahead and discover
     the sense of being still,
It is about self-exploration,
     choice and free will.

Stillness evokes an inner thirst,
     to explore deep beyond,
The connectedness to which
     we all tightly form a bond.
Learning to relax, to quiet the mind
     and become still,
Is a disciplined venture
     for the yearning to be filled.

Be filled with the splendor
       of the grandness deep inside,
Only you can find it within yourself,
       it doesn't try to hide.
Feel the sense of silence draw you
       to the center of who you are,
Your conscious awareness expands,
       feel yourself moving far.

Let yourself be with this moment,
       there are no limits at all,
It is your perception of what it is that colors
       or breaks your fall.
Quiet yourself now, be silent,
       journey inside far beyond,
Expand the illumination of your light,
       your radiance so fond.

Stillness is in the moment
       connecting universal ties,
When you sense discernment, release
       yourself, joyfully cry.
It is in the inner knowing
       that we are spiritually alive,
Celebrating the expansiveness within,
       as we continue to thrive.

Stillness. Quiet. Within. You are home.

Detachment

Does the body know the difference
　　　from "reality" and not?
Is it encoded in the cells generating a
　　　stronghold of the lot?
Can it hold the pain and discouragement,
　　　the grief and fear,
Resulting in an unconscious accumulation
　　　of sometimes years.

We don't even realize the effect
　　　our lives' woes create,
When we manifest illness trying
　　　to make the crooked straight.
Sometimes it is not a conscious act
　　　although it may seem,
Could we possibly make ourselves sick,
　　　maybe it's only a dream?

The different areas of the body, muscles
　　　and organs truly know,
That it is time to detach from guilt
　　　and allow love to grow.
What do we do about this powerful connection
　　　of body and mind?
Understand the delicate nature
　　　of attachment and the kind.

Holding on to resentment, anger, fear,
       and unconscious stuff,
Drives a deeper wedge in time
       until consciousness says enough!
Take the time to recognize your feelings,
       deal with them now,
It is in the present moment,
       where you feel empowered—POW!

Function from the core of your being,
       the essence of inner truth,
You will begin to release the pain, regardless
       of pudding or proof.
As you release the control of emotions
       that you gave power to,
Beyond you will find a new horizon
       for life to travel through.

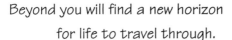

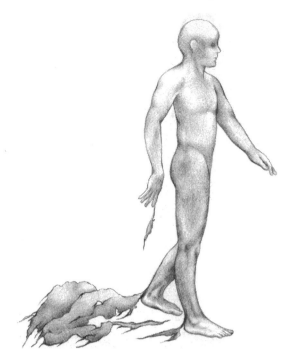

Detach from the grip of issues
    and fears, forgive and move on.
Release the attachments
    with which you have become so fond.
The material possessions
    and relationships just the same,
Can be detached through the love
    of the conscious choice game.

You will find that detachment brings freedom,
    unity, and space,
It encourages a sense of enlightenment
    illumined only by Grace.
Trust your inner guidance
    as you willingly detach and let go,
Be all that you are as you soar
    in the realization that you **do know**.

Conditioned Thoughts

Open up your vision to new beginnings now,
See how conditioned thoughts restrict and not allow.
They keep you locked up in your self-imposed chains,
As you struggle desperately to make personal gains.

These conditioned beliefs have been a part of your being,
Take the time to learn from them, eyes open wide for seeing.
Face them and embrace the fact that they exist in you,
Then have the willingness to erase them to create the new.

Conditioned thoughts may perpetuate insecurities and lack,
The control itself is conditioned, unaware of its tact.
Not feeling "good enough" is conditioning from the past,
Acknowledge these thoughts so they do not have to last.

While the ego nature is most resistant to change,
It is your spiritual unfoldment that compels you to arrange.
As you break up the old patterns conditioned within,
Your spiritualness will emerge to humbly win—

To win the essence that has always been a part of you,
Embrace the exhilaration of feeling whole and truly new.
Experience enlightenment deep within your core,
Step into your inner space, experience peace forevermore.

Synchronicity

The rightness of this moment falls into the lap of time
Not knowing where it's going, just trusting in the rhyme.

The synchronicity avails itself of the illusions to be
Detaching self of limitations to ethereal expansion so free.

Why would we believe that chance is a guiding light and force
Eliminating the moment's trust, a divinely assisted course?

The rightness delivered is of perfection, as we make our own choice
To follow the loving, stillness within, as we trust this inner voice.

The spontaneous presents itself in myriad ways for us to see,
That our spiritual essence will open the door, free of any key.

We own the knowledge, our birthright, to be all that we are
Honoring synchronicity, trusting, reaching far.

Dance in the gentle breeze, lifting as light as a kite,
Soar in the liberated expression of the eagle in flight.

It is in the serene knowingness that inner guidance
  impresses the heart.
As the synchronous dance of reality blends wholeness
  in all its parts.

The Self

Light of the heavens streams through the clouds
      tenderly touching the earth.
Reflecting the waters, drenching the soul,
      gracing the self of its worth.
The union of the self converges in synchronicity
      for its essence to be,
An age-old dance of the spirit,
      the mind extolling jubilant harmony.

The ego self angers at the tarnishing
      of its name,
While the essence self remains oh so humble
      just the same.
As the elemental self accepts the myriad
      of emotions expressed,
It is difficult for the ego to admit,
      see truth and confess.

The elemental self is the basic
      intuitive nature within.
The ego self is the personality
      in conflict always trying to win.
The essence self is the higher order
      within peacefully flying free,
Releasing the bondage of separate selves,
      creating wholeness in thee.

So the whole self is more than
      just a part of parts to see,
It is the Divine Essence awakening
      you to see the real "me."

Mirror Reflection

It is in the mirror reflection
      that I gain perspective to see,
That what I view in you,
      is what exists in me.

So funny this universal law
      teaches us to learn,
That life's lessons clarify
      with each and every turn.

As we make the choice
      to journey toward the whole,
We reflect off one another
      as we justify each and every toll.

What a blessing it is to see
      in you the real me,
This is how we awaken ourselves,
      to release, to expand, to be free.

A tenacious rendition of duality
       exists in the guarded fear,
As we attach to our thoughts,
       through our shielded tears.

Sharing from the heart of compassion,
       the love of our souls,
Revealing the Essence of our Truth,
       to gain knowledge, detaching past roles.

So clear the virtue of the self,
       bounces from this being,
Presenting life's lessons, enlightening the
       self, transforming inner seeing.

Purpose

Every moment in life is purpose-filled,
As we let go and trust in the ALL.
Directing thought in peaceful willingness,
Subconsciously guiding the fall.

To lift oneself up is in the notion,
Of knowing it's not wrong or right.
To experience freedom in space and motion,
Moving unencumbered without a fight.

It is a gentle echoed knowingness,
With which we choose to act.
To live a life in stateful bliss,
Creating purpose regardless of fact.

A fact is in the outer reality,
Of which we merely exist.
It is in our inner existence,
Of how we truly subsist.

Yes, our lives' lessons are real,
As we awaken to the intention.
We mindfully choose to listen and feel,
Our lives' purpose and true direction.

Gateway II

Recondition the Self

Renew to Thee

*"When we surrender to our essence, which is
connected to the whole universe, we resonate with
the whole and pull to us all that is needed."*
— Gloria D. Karpinski
"Where Two Worlds Touch"

To recondition the self, embrace the reality of what is
and the illusion of what isn't. To think Truth everyday
is to know reality in our true Essence. Truth is a
silent principle. You can learn to silence the noise and mind
chatter (illusion) and listen to the silent law that speaks
from the True Self within (reality). What you are doing is
training the intellect to the passageway of "understanding."
After you begin to embrace the essence of all that you are in
wholeness, truth and knowledge come forth.

To recondition the self is to recognize and remove layers of
illusion in character. You then can begin to release the
character of false thinking that causes the dis-ease of
humankind. What is held in thought, in the heart, in prayer
and faith, will manifest. As you acknowledge the positive
perspective of living a life of simplicity, happiness and love, so
shall it be. Shifting my consciousness to right thinking has
given me a light, free, positive formula toward daily living.

Reconditioning the self is a commitment to seeking the
essence of the soul. Preparatory stages toward the
unconditioned self are initiated to clear oneself of impurities
and balance the mindbody. To recondition oneself is to hold
firm to truth, to love unconditionally and to demonstrate
equality.

As you climb the mountain and ponder your ascension, you
will recondition the old cycles and patterns. A newness
grows through an emptying out—a replenishing of clarity and

Recondition the self to—

- Embrace the personal healing process
- Free the mind of attachment
- Still the emotional body
- Relax, nourish and nurture the physical body
- Ignite your inner flame
- Rekindle the sense of wholeness possible within
- Create a more fulfilling positive reality
- Live a purposeful, conscious, giving, loving, caring life
- Seek and discover your Goodness and your Truth

clear intention. To continue your journey up the mountain, your inner sights will continue to awaken a balance in your mental, emotional and physical bodies. You can't help but to achieve an equilibrium of self as you attend to the self and become aware of what is and what isn't. You know. You just know when you listen with inner ears and feel from your heart center. When you begin living life from this vantage point, you will never turn back. The climb up the mountain may appear steep. Yet, in truth, it is a mere twinkling of God's eyes guiding you home.

self-expansion

Reality or Illusion?

Look in the distance and what do you see?
A merging of the heavens and earth in reality.
But when you reach this point far off,
Once a goal-oriented view becomes an illusion aloft.

So how does illusion and reality really compare?
Is it like a mind free of thought, not being aware?
Or is it releasing the contrived world of form,
Like when you blend a hot and cold, the end result, warm.

Is our reality keenly objective in all that we see?
Or do we narrow our focus to passively agree.
To broaden our perspective defies the social norm,
That the mental image of thought is illusion in form.

Don't take this notion seriously as you will come to find,
That everything is an illusion, it will boggle your mind.
Although the world of form seems solid, please guess again,
It's all made up of waves and particles, why, what, and when.

It is the power we give to things creating a grandiose scheme,
Just try to release association of thoughts as you drift in dream.
Keep yourself uplifted in consciousness, in the neutral space,
Whether reality or illusion, it's about living in love and grace.

Objective Reality

What is this objective reality all about?
Can it really encourage harmony without a doubt?
Does it expand your inner awareness beyond,
Where edges of your consciousness unify and bond?

It is in the realm of simplicity that we begin to see,
That our objective reality is all possibilities to be.
Realize that life is more than embracing black and white,
It is the space of choice between the difference of left and right.

The space between opposites gives us room to grow,
It creates an open awareness of possibilities to know.
Our objective reality permits us to expand from within,
Learning lessons not from failure, nor expectation to win.

It is the gentle reminder that possibility does exist,
To look at every situation with choices you can enlist.
It is not in the either-or thinking that you need to adhere,
Rather the lighthearted acknowledgment of releasing the fear.

Fear embeds the cellular level, resisting the seed of change,
Hanging, clinging, grasping tightly to familiar cycles arranged.
Our emotions can paralyze us, inhibiting our ability to grow,
Living from objective reality creates opportunity to experience flow.

Close your eyes and envision a cube on the screen of your mind,
What are you looking for and exactly what do you find?
Do you see more than one side of this dimensional form?
Or are you stuck in a pattern, like fear erupting from a storm.

It is your objective reality that allows you the choice to see
There are many sides to this cube, the possibilities are up to thee.
Learn to create balance, harmony and a free-spirited vision,
Embracing the reality that life is possibility and indeterminate decision.

Truth

Trust in the now
It is the point to be.
You must let go and allow,
For all of you to see.

It is not about what was,
Or what is going to be.
It is the present because,
You are you, a part of me.

Forget about what others say,
Or how they look at you.
Be in your Truth each day,
Embrace the Presence as new.

Feel the gentle whisper
Of guidance within your heart.
It is a sense of deep reliance,
That is close rather than apart.

The Truth is hidden within your soul
As you have come to know.
That life's journey is not a goal,
But the unfolding self to grow.

The Simple

It's pure. It's basic. It's undeniably sweet.
It's the mellow encounter; it's very discreet.
It's life at the center, the original plan.
Made to be simple, not the complexity of man.

How do we fall into the trap of confusion?
Is it stress, as we obsess over the illusion
That life is meant to be struggle and strain,
To be filled with anxiety, judgment and pain?

Release these intentions; it doesn't have to be.
Retrain your brain to live happily and free.
Step off that mountain and soar unencumbered,
Your entire life can be filled with awe and wonder.

The secret of life is defined by the One,
To embrace Truth and enjoy the simplicity in fun.
It's the element of the simple that we may come to find,
To redefine the basics in the love and life of humankind.

Light

I AM THE LIGHT OF MY TRUTH,
As it is the Way of the Way.
It is the call of being,
To be acknowledged each new day.

It is in the unspoken word,
Where the radiance of inner light shines.
It is all in what you have heard,
With lovingness and Truth Divine.

The message of light is yours ...

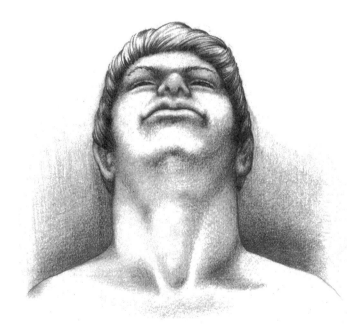

Listen

Listen to the call of nature
       from the forest's floor,
Blades of grass conversing, dancing,
       growing evermore.
Gently nestle into the bedlike grass, relax,
       feel free,
Softly close your eyes, be silent,
       just listen and see.

Your mental and emotional being
       creates pictures within,
It is your spiritual essence
       that hears the drop of a pin.
Learn to use discernment
       as you go deep into relaxation,
Eliminate expectation
       and simply be with all creation.

If you choose to pray
       to the Source of your Being,
You are willingly talking,
       there is no seeing.
As you deliberately enter
       into a relaxed and calm state,
You open your inner ears for a still, quiet voice,
       patiently await.

As you courageously journey down
      your life's path to find
That it is straight and narrow,
      it doesn't deviate or wind.
It is in the nature of knowingness
      that makes it simple, not complex,
Feel and sense the impression within,
      listen for guidance next.

Feel the lush grass around you,
      the breeze massaging your face,
Know when Truth is upon thee,
      you will be filled with Grace.
The realization of Oneness
      is an illumination of the soul,
As the concept of yourself expands,
      you will release all roles.

You will begin to let go of the labels
      and roles you have taken on,
You will open yourself up to freely express
      from a space far beyond.
Listen for Truth in your heart,
      the gift of unfoldment is yours
The Dominion expresses through Spirit,
      it lovingly opens doors.

Listen with your inner ears now,
get silent and go inside,
Await the communion of Truth,
within you it peacefully resides.
Be patient, love yourself, fill yourself up
with respect and compassion.
The expression of Truth reveals itself
in right time and right action.

Clarity

This poem is meant for you,
  as I hold you in my mind,
I realize your thoughts are racing
  as you search to seek or find,
That clarity in seeing is masked
  by the world of form,
Of what we've grown to know as societal
  and cultural norms.

Although your will expresses weakness
       by the gripping vultures of past,
Please make the conscious choice to break
       patterns, they don't have to last.
Fear is the greatest obstacle
       to clarity in your life,
Reason with your consciousness, free yourself,
       eliminate the strife.

Create the vision in your head
       of exactly what you desire,
Even though this is ego-based,
       it will ignite your inner fire.
To reach deep down to the core of being,
       your Essence graciously speaks,
Through your personality it recognizes
       all you'll find as you seek.

Clarify your purpose now, embrace
       the cavern's depth inside,
It is all you are in this unconditional love
       by which you truly abide.
Surrender, release, accept what was,
       it is time to be ALL you,
It is in this knowingness of clarity
       you will find the greatest gift,
       YOU!

Forgiveness

Forgiveness is a word
    I truthfully extol
Releasing emotional attachment,
    awakening reality of my soul.

Forgiveness delivers my shielded heart
    far beyond its norm,
Uplifting beingness from judgment, doubt,
    how to conform.

The reality of forgiveness
      is a knowing I do find,
The essence of my being,
      pureness of heart and mind.

I forgive myself and others now,
      for it is of the past.
I unlock the hold of relentless thought,
      I willing thou cast.

The heart of forgiveness lovingly
      disintegrates illusions of old.
While my faith in the moment's light,
      guides peace and love to unfold.

As I forgive, I surrender
      to the highest of Thee
Freeing myself to gain clarity
      in the vision of what is "to be."

As I now forgive, the nature
      of balance settles within my core,
I neutralize life's ebb and flow,
      accepting myself forevermore.

As I forgive, I free myself to live.

Angel Wings

It is sometimes difficult to recognize
    the one with elegant wings,
The kind that when outstretched
    embrace the heavens that sing.
These wings glide freely
    in the breeze of Divine Grace,
Soaring, floating, suspended
    in the magnificence of infinite space.

The wings of an angel display
    great honor and trust,
They encourage love and harmony
    to all with a must.
The wings of an angel will gently guide you
    through your day,
As you learn to be accepting,
    knowing the answer is in the Way.

The angels want your goodness
        to be expressed from your core,
Now trust in their guidance,
        rather than question what they are for.
The wings of an angel will offer you a lesson,
        not a free ride,
To practice flying freely,
        after grasping the toss of a turbulent tide.

An angel is filled with lightheartedness,
        laughter and fun,
Smile with your angels and recognize
        your connectedness to the One.
It is in the guidance of your angels
        as you come to know,
That you are an angel too, learning
        and yearning to grow.

Can you take your angel wings
        and spread them open wide?
To allow the essence of yourself,
        the core of being inside,
To reveal your truth and expression
        that uniquely is you,
Through the angelic realm of illumination,
        brilliant and new.

Surrender

Energy stirs in my core to awaken
      the sleep-filled dark
A grand illumination, a self-realization
      recognizing my angel's hark.
I encounter deep trust to let go
      and reveal what is erupting in me
To free myself of guilt and fear,
      the root system I clearly see.

My depths of knowingness loosen within
      for conditions to release,
I acknowledge the emotions as they surface,
      honor them and feel peace.
Sometimes I make the choice to feel it again,
      forgive myself and be,
Open in my heart, free in mind,
      my spirit available to be all of me.

I am all that I am, lovingly connected
      to Universal Source
Expanding conscious awareness,
      sharing my true course.
As I surrender and forgive,
      I detach and rise above,
I embrace serenity and freedom now,
      the truth of unconditional love.

Lightheartedness

Lift it, open it, light it up—free yourself to soar.
Expand your heart in spontaneity, leap as you explore.
Feel the gentle heart of the playful child inside,
Expressing laughter in the cheer to seek or to hide.

Lightheartedness is being lifted in a light, fun way
Like the luminescent rising sun of each new day.
As you awaken to the presence of lightness, fresh and free,
Be lovingly and consciously aware for all of you to be.

You can lightly break the patterns of days and years past,
Open yourself to expansiveness, sheer balance and the vast.
You are filled with light and laughter in your happy heart
Bathing in the moment's space, releasing associations in part.

Reach high and stretch yourself, grasping a cloud above,
Pull yourself up, float freely as you fly with the white dove.
Feel the lightness of your life with an unencumbered sense,
Granting yourself possibilities, being relaxed rather than tense.

With this peaceful, light heart comes great compassion,
Share your virtues with others, guiding their conscious action.
You are this lighthearted being as you express from your core
That nothing matters but right now, no less or no more.

Pay attention to the lightness in each present moment today,
Freeing yourself from limited living, expanding how you may.
Lightheartedness has always been an integral part of you,
Express your heart lightly, transform the old you into the new.

Inner Guidance

Be all that you are,
It is not hard to be.
The distance may seem far,
But you are really ready to be free.

Your inner guidance is there for you,
Get silent and go within.
Be prepared for change through and through,
Trust and believe it is a win, win.

These messages will continue to come,
As you prepare for your life's work.
It will provide support and encourage which from,
Denial and suppression may lurk.

That's all for now as you can see,
The message is quite clear.
You must persist and reveal the "Me,"
And release every bit of fear.

Yes, you are on your way now,
For others to watch from afar.
Stay centered as in the way of the Tao,
And you will teach people who you really are.

Inner Life

An extraordinary sensation filters
　　through the bodymind so pure
Rushing from the toe to head,
　　connecting the dimensions as it were.
A heightened knowing, an inner rhythm
　　coupled deep and beyond,
Part of the gentle consciousness
　　of love and light so fond.

The presence of oneness engulfs each cell,
    emerging, expanding within,
A transmutation of body and mind
    releasing impartation in.
This state of being is lifted above
    the human world of thought,
Purely one global song,
    a liberating expression caught.

Be in the plenitude of Grace
    streaming far and free
Renewing your oneness with every aspect
    of you and me to Thee.
The healing blessing bestowed upon your heart,
    your soul and mind
Integrates in stillness as you detach
    from thought of any kind.

The instantaneous moment
    is enlightened through your trust
Communing in the blissful essence,
    free of shoulds or musts.
Let go the world of thought
    to open yourself to be
Expanding your sense of self with the Source
    in all of thee.

The rhythm of the inner life flourishes
    beyond time and space
Free of projection in mind, living truth,
    from the heart, in Grace.

Be and Receive

It is in the gift of receiving that we come to know,
That love embraces us fully as we allow ourselves to grow.
To receive is to be accepting, sincere, and truly humble—
Open your arms to all! Cease the fumble in the tumble.

As you share your light through the windows of your being,
Allow others to give to you to enhance and enlighten your seeing.
Your path is paved in clarity as you allow it all to unfold,
Hold on to your truth, for your Essence will be told.

It is in the gift of receiving that we learn how to share.
To give from the heart without a question or a dare.
It is time for your awareness to direct itself in truth,
You are whole in yourself now, watch the unveiling, it's the proof.

Balance

It is in the midpoint of opposites,
That we gain perspective to view
Our life as a vision of wholeness,
That is peaceful, healthy and new.

Through the principle of duality,
Can we truly come to learn
The creativeness in our reality,
As we teeter, totter and turn.

The midpoint of opposites is balance,
As we search in the to and fro.
Engaging in life's mystical dance,
To embrace what our spirits truly know.

It is not in the either-or thought,
Nor the neither-this-nor-that thinking,
That we experience the space of neutrality
Creating upliftment, keeping us from sinking.

You will find in this space of freedom
A life crystallized in clarity and bliss,
To discover the gentle balance of life from
Unfoldment of wholeness, which is neither
that nor this.

It Is What it Is

The moment of truth is captured
      in the unspoken word.
It is revealed from the heart,
       intrinsically felt, not heard.
This knowingness is embellished
      upon the consciousness walls,
Expressing the impression
      of reality's hidden falls.

So difficult it is to escape
      illusions here and now,
Accept the knowledge of inner guidance,
      release, expand, allow.
The voice of reason may temptingly alter
      your decision to act,
Yet the allowance of the unspoken word jousts
      with brilliant tact.

Aha! You project from your
      love-sustaining heart,
The magnificence of rightness acknowledged
      from the start.
The windows of the eyes
      see the truth as it is,
It cannot hide the essence of the soul,
      it is what it is.

Honor

Pause for a moment to recognize
        the space in your heart,
That which represents "respect," reflecting
        the greater sum of parts.
This deep respect conveys acceptance
        of the self with love,
It awakens to a higher sense of awareness
        from above.

To honor from above, below, outside
        and all around,
It starts from the heart, the essence
        so profound.
Take a step within yourself and feel
        the greatness in
The expansiveness of your soul,
        the Infinite therein.

Take a ride on the wings of glory, floating,
        gliding free,
Claim the goodness in your heart, owning,
        honoring thee.
Open yourself, be more aware, experience
        magnificence now,
Opportunity is awaiting you, honor it,
        lovingly allow.

Honor your body, your soul
      and your mind,
A vision of balance and harmony
      you will find.
Bring forth from within a spark
      of your being,
Honor your inner guidance, a reflection
      of your seeing.

Honor all that you are,
      rest in contemplation.
Reach and touch the brightest star,
      embrace the elation.
You are deserving of all the love
      buried in your soul,
Accept, respect, and honor this,
      it's your birthright, not a goal.

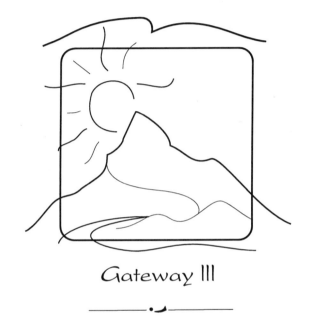

Gateway III

The Unconditioned Self

Come to Be

"There is no need to run outside for better seeing . . .
nor to peer from a window. Rather abide at the center of
your being; for the more you leave it, the less you learn.
Search your heart and see . . . if [s/he] is wise who takes
each turn; the way to do is to be."

— Lao Tzu
"The Way of Life"

Awaken to the realization that all is Spirit and in
Spirit there is no disharmony. Here, you live as your
True Self. You have let go of the dream or illusion of
what you thought you were, to truly be all that you are in
your essence. Now, when Truth is spoken, recognize it as the
Essence of ALL; the One Being; the realization of the unity of
God, the Universe, the Infinite and humankind. This is Truth.
To commune in the stillness of silence is to reach your hand
forth and lift yourself up to this knowingness. It is Light. It
is Love. It is Knowledge. It is Presence. It is all that you are
in ALL that you are. Your intellect does not heal you; only
the integrative union of your soul being and your personal
being heals.

The Essence of ALL is omnipotent, omniscient, and
omnipresent. We are one in this great Field of Essence. Just
be in it. Be still and be ... in the Essence of wholeness and
the Oneness therein. In this process, we evolve into the light
of understanding and become spiritually awakened.

the self realized

The Unconditioned Self—

- Experiences the Divine Universal Presence

- Is in the eternal present moment

- Accepts and trusts that the best will find you

- Lovingly holds up the world in a global conscious effort to heal, to love, to be

- Experiences a limitless, boundless reality of what is

- Accepts a world of perpetual change and doesn't get caught up in it

- Experiences the lighthearted essence of Spirit

- Shares evolvement and enlightenment with others

- Makes the self available to the Essence of ALL that is

- Contemplates, meditates and becomes still to know True Wisdom

Transformation

To seek personal transformation
        is manifesting change within,
Carefully consider all parts of being
        then proceed to go in.
Initiating this course of action
        is acknowledgment at your core,
You realize you are more than human,
        step through the ethereal door.

To change oneself is to honor all that resides
        in the depths of being,
Refocus from the outer world toward
        the inner sense of seeing.
This place of all knowing is the divine, intuitive
        spiritual home
From which we walked away
        independently on the roam.

No need to search any longer
        for truth is beating in your heart,
It has always danced with your beingness
        right from the start.
The truth is you as this spiritual being,
        awaiting the journey back,
Embrace the Essence of ALL that Is,
        grasping the eternal track.

You will transform your mental
      and emotional self, physical being too,
Own all that you are right now,
      as you lovingly release to renew.
Conditioned patterns lose power,
      the ego's purpose no longer is in view
The secret of life's happiness
      has always been within you.

When the unfoldment of Truth
      tenderly guides you through the gate
It is your spirit lovingly exclaiming
      it is never too late.
This is the journey, the inner path
      you've discovered deep in your core,
Share this knowingness with others now,
      be in your Allness forevermore.

body   mind   emotions   spirit

To Be

The nature of wholeness
      is in the learning to be,
It is in the present moment
      as we use discernment to see.

The gracious gift of the Essence of ALL
      reveals in the now,
As we lovingly, patiently,
      await to allow.

To allow the omniscient, still voice
      of the blessed guidance within,
Bestow upon our beingness,
      peace and love deep in.

Thus, "Being" is the Divine Life
      of heaven here on earth,
Unfolding in the process is our expansion
      of self, service and worth.

Lao Tzu eloquently expressed,
      "the way to do is to be,"
Kindling our inner beingness to forgive,
      be truth-filled, feel free.

Once we harken to the state of beingness
in our every day,
The act of doing will gently follow
in a unified, harmonic way.

"To Be" is to release the intention
of any wrong or right,
Holding in our hearts the present stillness
of the light.

"To Be" is to dissolve association
in the laws of duality,
Recognizing the Spirit in all,
love's arms embracing reality.

So it is in the realm of "Being"
that lifts our hearts and souls,
"To Be" liberated in a timeless reality,
detached from the drama of control.

Awareness Rising

No matter how difficult it may seem
    to acknowledge who you are,
Remember the roots from whence you came,
    eternity is now, not afar.

Your spiritual beingness is yearning
    to be recognized by all of you,
To have you embrace the depth of your soul,
    and say to the highest, yes I do.

Do you recognize your soul and connectedness
    to the generous One?
To respect and honor the healing art
    of all daughters and sons.

Conscious awareness is rising
    as you lift your essence to speak,
Knowing the Divine and the One
    are all a part of the courageous and meek.

Trust with your heart as you expand your sense
    of all that you are
It is in the powerful, loving moment you are
    guided by the Light's luminescent star.

Release the conditions that pull you
    in resisting the thought of change,
Allow the brilliance of Essence
    as you joyfully lift and arrange.

To detach from the old patterns
        as you create newness far in,
Is to believe the truth in reality
        as your existence is not about sin.

For sin is an earthly creation
        that was given power to,
Now it is time to change the moment
        to love and share through and through.

Yes, it is the simple plan
        as it was meant to be,
To move through what is necessary for you
        and then you will agree.

Your conscious awareness is rising
        as your level of spirituality shines,
Now share your Truth with others
        as you renew the hope in Thine.

Unfoldment

Unfoldment is the gentle whisper
      of Infinite God guiding you
It is the silent knowingness of how to act,
      what to do.
The action comes from the message
      far and deep within,
Only you can recognize it if you are mindful
      as you go in.

The tendency to direct your own course
      and make a human choice,
Disregards the essence of unfoldment delivered
      from the inner voice.
The difference from intellectual reasoning
      and unfolding deep inside,
Is the security of conditioned thought
      not the trust of your inner guide.

I know it may seem difficult to make sense
      of this at first,
Free your mind of conditioned patterns,
      allow yourself to thirst.
Open yourself up freely to the meaning
      of all that you are,
Feel yourself, indulge in the moment's brilliance,
      you will reach far.

Do not be afraid of the gloriousness
          that is a part of you
Allow yourself to experience the present,
          a vision clear and new.
It is trust and patience in the unfolding process
          here on earth,
Guided through the ethereal heavens planted
          in your soul at birth.

Yes, you can acknowledge the grandness
          of all you truly are,
Believe, have faith, release the doubt,
          reveal your radiant star.
When it is unfolded unto you,
          follow the lead of the Light,
You will be humbly awakened,
          embracing inner peace and inner sight.

I Miss You

The sadness swells in my body as I allow the tears to release.
I realize my friend's spirit is soaring freely this moment in peace.

I sigh, I let go, I cry, I do whatever impresses my heart.
I see, I feel, I know Essence of Spirit guides me as it imparts.

I incarnate, I live, I rebirth, time and time again.
I evolve in my essence, seeking wisdom and mastery to ascend.

I anchor into the Truth of Spirit, unconsciously relaxing my breath.
I fear not the transition of life, the unfolding process of death.

I cannot help my thoughts of you as I reach out my hands
        to feel.
To acknowledge your presence, which is gone, no longer
        physically real.

I lovingly hold your memory in my mind, as my heart
        gallantly adjusts to the new.
I carry on in the moment's light as I'm surrounded
        in an angelic, white healing hue.

I miss you.

Soar freely.

Compassionate Detachment

In the loving embrace of Spirit,
      we mend the heart of its fear.
In it is the Divine Rightness, as we
      release the relentless past years.

As we open ourselves to unfoldment,
      we see Truth in the eyes of Grace.
It is this compassionate detachment
      that heals and renews our inner space.

From this place of transformative rebirth,
      a new perspective flourishes in thee.
Gleaned from the loving detachment of
      what was honorably a part of me.

Through our insightful acknowledgment
      we have gained a vision to see,
That our compassionate detachment is
      about self-acceptance and respect, as
      we lovingly set ourselves free.

Suspend Yourself
and Relax

Suspend yourself in the buoyant blue waters,
      floating on the edge with ease,
Embrace upon your face the peaceful massage,
      the healing effect of the breeze.
Give into gravity, relax deep in
      as your mind and body lie adrift.
Feel the release, trust in the waters,
      the acceptance and support of this gift.

It is the beauty of the waters absorbed
      through your loving and clear essence
That creates a harmonic convergence,
      enlightening your true presence.
As the melodious rhythm of nature's way
      lulls you far and beyond,
A simultaneous flow in communion
      generates inner joy so fond.

Embrace this place through unfoldment
      suspended in you so free,
The awakening of your true self,
      honoring and accepting all of thee.
Relax ...

Communion With Thee

Oh, Divine Spirit, you lovingly placed
in our minds to see
That all of life's lessons bring us back
to be with thee.

Oh, Divine Spirit, you purely placed
in our hearts to feel,
Challenging our awareness to know
what is illusion and what is real.

You have given us the opportunity
to be in conflict at the ego's request,
To experience the mesmerizing state
of the delusional self, the obsessed.

To be in Your love is to embrace Truth,
       Compassion, and the One,
Releasing the control and power
       of the little self on the run.

We stand away to serenely observe
       the life that we lead,
To allow ourselves tranquil living
       as we plant the simplicity seed.

The perceptions from the ego-base
       are tainted from conditions past,
Continuing the whirlwind drama of illusion,
       how long will this last?

Interpretations are the ego's powerful grip
       on the mind,
Strangling our vision of reality and love
       of nature and the kind.

To be all that we are
       is to awaken to Your pure love,
Built into our genetic code,
       linked to You within and above.

We shan't take this message lightly
       for it is time to be whole,
Acknowledging our essence,
       releasing the past, freeing our holy souls.

We are intuitively guided to start fresh now,
       the cause is for us to see,
That it is about our connection with ALL,
       for us to be in communion with Thee.

I Am

I Am the breath you take in as you fill your core with grace.

I Am the light of heaven drawing illumination to your face.

I Am the beautiful eagle soaring strongly across the skies.

I Am the fury in the heart of the lonely one who cries.

I Am the narrow vision stretching itself to expand.

I Am the meager fallacy searching for truth so grand.

I Am the lesson in everything, opportunity to listen and learn.

I Am the vibrant reality as you unfold with every turn.

I Am the lavender-laced mountain, upon me you awaken with awe.

I Am the knowingness reflected through the eyes you longingly saw.

I Am the lifted presence you felt as you were so still.

I Am the Truth of all, I Am acknowledged through your free will.

I Am ALL that I Am. I Am the Light of your truth.

I Am the Essence of all, a life of love you live as my proof.

I Am.

The Essence of Spirit

Elaborate textures reveal themselves as you sift
through the rough and the pure,
Elevating your awareness to recognize the
pious posture's allure.
Brilliance lives within your heart to be awakened
in the moment's light.
It is your generous illumined self making the
dark sunshine bright.

It is the nature of wholeness that speaks from
your individual soul,
In the search for communion with Spirit,
the Truth, and embracing your role.
Your vision gets blurred by the illusion of
dragons in the night,
Although they appear to be in dream state,
always seek out the light.

It is the Spirit of ALL filling you with
dignity, grace and love,
You must recognize, intuit, and feel what
is or isn't from above.
It is in the gentle knowingness that we
guide you from deep in,
It is your alert perception that is felt
as if razor thin.

The Light and the Way are provided to you
as you journey long and far,
Deliverance in the Essence of Spirit is your
eternal gift and guiding star.
As you awaken to the message that "I AM
forever the Light of your Truth,"
You will understand betrayal of the fittest
and the loyalty and love as my proof.

Allow the warmth and tender surround of
Grace's wings so free
To lovingly engage themselves as they lift
and honor all of thee.
Secure and special, the message of Truth
befalls upon all of you,
Cultivating and creating clarity, a vision
of what you are to do.

The Light, the Truth, the Essence of Spirit
that I AM directing your hand,
Releasing the pull of gravity, expanding
consciousness in every grain of sand.
Open your heart and feel the reminder of love's dew
caress your lip,
You will taste and feel the greatness in the
reality of this life's trip.

Feel the Flow of Spirit

The veils of illusion appear impermeable,
      as we blindly find our way
To the knowing reality underneath
      the external conditioned day.

As we step outside ourselves to serenely
      observe True Presence,
Our awareness is awakened by the
      claimed belief of lack and absence.

Conscious awareness rises as we pursue
      our realization of the ALL,
Journeying deep within ourselves,
      guided in the search after the fall.

As we fell away from the Essence of all
      that we were to be,
We've become enlightened to the ancient
      wisdom that we are a part of Thee.

To dance in the Essence of Oneness is a
      glorifying, mystifying waltz.
Flowing in the fluidity of Truth, releasing
      seduction of the false.

Embrace now and sense the impression,
  the God-realization in the still.
Feel and absorb this knowingness
  at the core of your own will.

Realize mental thoughts cannot bring
  forth the communing of ALL,
It is in the loving acknowledgment of
  unfoldment in the Truth of your call.

As you resist the ego-thought that there is
  only one way to see,
Rightness and knowingness is the alchemy
  of awareness for you to truly "be."

So expand your concept of self as you
  open your heart to feel
That the flow of Spirit in communion
  is not justified, it's a knowingness
  that is Real.

Pure Love

Love is a knowing energy that we share as we
    open our guarded hearts to be.
Love is a quenched thirst that continues to flow
    unobstructed and carefree.
Love carries the light of the heart
    to enliven the spirit in humankind.
Love encourages the hopeless as they discover
    brilliance in their body and mind.
Love dances deep in as it awakens
    an intention to be filled.
Love expands our awareness to the limitless
    potential we are willed.
Love is steeped in gratitude for our
    exchange seems so unreal.
To touch, to taste, to go beyond that
    which expresses what we feel.
Love is a knowledge, an unfiltered wisdom
    untouched by human error.
It acknowledges our innocence and invulnerability
    as we unconditionally care.
Love is the Divine knowing that we are
    here to be,
One in the same, hand-in-hand, reaching to
    the highest degree.

Love is pure. Love is the supreme flow of energy
          unencumbered in motion and bliss.
It has no limits because it is the
          Great Source of pure beingness.
Love.
          Be it. Give it. Receive it. Allow it.
Allow love's compassion to permeate
          every cell of the whole and feel it.
Just get in touch with the heart center's
          flutter in the rush of love's pure tide.
It expands the synchronous moment into stillness,
          a trust-filled knowing we abide.
So the dainty trickle of a succulent dew drop
          moistens the earth with love,
It continues to share its delight to bare
          its essence from nature above.
Yes, love is nature, an energy,
          an unknowable unified presence.
Love is you through and through.
          It is your true essence.
Pure love.

The Moon

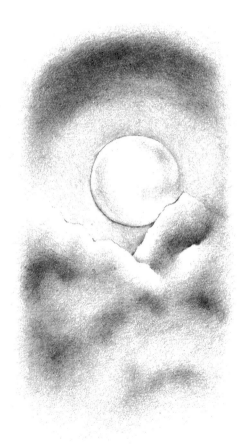

Moon so bright
An incredible sight
Jewel so high
Majesty of sky

Drift far away
Bathe in the rays
Energy moving through
Create change anew

How to describe
The feeling that resides
Deep in my heart
Nurturing all parts

A healing illumination
An earthly creation
Delivering its essence
A mystifying presence

Gaze into space
Galaxy in place
Take yourself home
Dream, wander, roam.

Believe Me
When I Say I Am ....

Believe me when I say I am feeling the world's despair.
Believe me when I say I am discovering that
   many do care.

Believe me when I say I am envisioning a world of love.
Believe me when I say I am crystallizing inner strength
      from above.

Believe me when I say I am praying for world peace.
Believe me when I say I am encouraging people
      to release.

Believe me when I say I am enlightened by your gaze.
Believe me when I say I am touched
      by your ways.

Believe me when I say I am revealing my inner essence.
Believe me when I say I am acknowledging
      your true presence.

Believe me when I say I am searching from inside myself.
Believe me when I say I am visioning
      for everyone's good health.

Believe me when I say I am teaching from my heart.
Believe me when I say I am trying
      to finish what I start.

Believe me when I say I am guided by the Spirit of All.
Believe me when I say I am confident
      to learn from the fall.

Believe me when I say I am living in the angels' glow.
Believe me when I say I am harmonizing
      with all I truly know.

The Nature of God

The luminescent sun appears
  cresting the canyon wall
Projecting upon the red sandstone
  its expansive image so tall.

Convoluted structures of magnificent stone
  so strong
Surround the water's edge as fish dance
  and birds hymn their sweet song.

As I sit afloat the water,
  centered in the canyon's delight,
The vision of what I see can only be measured
  by God's insight.

This masterful creation has evolved
  from the highest indeed,
It's magnificence a revelation of a peace-filled
  moment planted as a seed.

I listen to love's echo resonate deep
  in these beauteous walls,
Lauded in all its holiness, I embrace Truth,
  the essence of God's call.

The attainment of the
mountainous summit
is to discover the "True Self."

Afterword

Synthesizing this information may come naturally to you or it may be a struggle. Either way you look at it, it has stimulated some type of shift in your consciousness. Listen within yourself and experience the guidance from your heart and soul. You may have begun to experience a more open, nonjudgmental awareness. You may have begun to acknowledge the present moment as the nectar of living. You may have found that you are not getting caught up in the trivial, for the trivial is merely a blip in all of reality. You may have found your mirror reflection in a friend with whom you have made a deep connection. You may even have found yourself embracing the beauty of the butterfly's symmetry in flight or being awestruck by the sight of a lavendar-laced mountainscape.

The shift in your consciousness is now taking you to new heights within yourself. You now may own the realization that you are an incredible being, spiritually and humanly. The radiance of your light and essence can reveal itself, as you completely accept your goodness with no conditions attached. You may have found that loving detachment through trust and faith will carry you lightly through the ethereal gateway. The neutral space between opposites has given you a new sense of freedom, unity, spontaneity, nonjudgment, unification, equality, and unconditional love. With the lessons you have learned and are learning, you are becoming more comfortable with it all. Applying these lessons into daily living is about uniting your external and internal worlds. As you continue to challenge the veils of illusion in the outer world, it will blend with the reality of your inner world, once again providing balance within the whole.

You have learned to listen within yourself and follow your inner guidance. Further contemplate these poems as you need, glancing at them at times, completely immersing yourself in them at others. Your intuitive self will continue to expand as you make space within to grow (to empty out). There is no right or wrong in it, it just is. In this, you will continue to make choices, learn personal lessons, expand your awareness and realize your sense of connectedness to it ALL.

The words, the verse, the energy within this book are soully for enhancing your conscious awareness to your nature of being whole in mind, body, heart and soul. If I have touched you in a somewhat curious, mystical way, then I am sincerely grateful for sharing my experiences with you. If you find that you are unaffected by the contents of this book, I am sincerely grateful for that, too. Your life's path will direct itself in perfect synchronicity to achieve your life's purpose. However, whatever, wherever you are on your path, accept, honor, forgive and love yourself unconditionally. The Source of your Being is gently guiding your hand. Just reach inside, climb the mountain, seek your Essence and embrace the Nature of Being Whole.

Key Concepts

affirmation — A personal, positive statement, written in the present tense "as if" it has occurred, that embodies a purpose or a goal. When repeated several times, these directed energies of positive thought will reprogram the conscious mind. Affirmations are used to balance and heal the mental body. You will find them dispersed throughout this book.

angelic — Referring to the kingdom of angels, which is unlike the human kingdom in that they are invisible. They serve to manifest Divine Impression through human form. This realm guides, directs and compassionately unfolds an intelligent deliverance of Universal Wisdom as messengers of the Essence of ALL/God.

atonement — At-one-ment is the state of Oneness reflecting unity and harmony in humankind and Universal Source.

attachment — The hidden vice of the ego that holds tight to the illusion of form. This illusion creates a thick veil over the eyes and heart to inhibit insight. Right thought, acceptance, and forgiveness encourages illumination, thus loving detachment of the thoughtform.

beingness — "-ness" meaning state or degree, hence it is the full state of being; the encompassing of all essence; accepting and honoring all that is around and throughout the self.

centered — A state of inner balance merging the physical, mental, emotional and spiritual bodies in well-being.

compassion — The synthesized aspect of wisdom and love, unconditionally delivered.

consciousness — Meaning "mind with knowledge," it is the combined result of the intellect and matter integrated and synthesized into a focused awareness. To expand the sense of consciousness is to know within oneself what cannot be physically recognized; a subjective recognition of subtle truth and intuitive awareness.

contemplation — Using the mental body to hold steady a mental device, word or thoughtform and serenely observe the unlimited possibilities; simply "being" in the present moment and watching with inner vision and listening with inner ears.

detachment — Freeing ourselves from the hidden voice of the ego that is holding tight to the illusion of form. Through right thinking, acceptance and forgiveness, **loving detachment** removes the veils that inhibit insight, thus encouraging illumination.

dis-ease — A sense of disharmony and fragmentation reflected in the lower-self triad; the uncomfortable nature oftentimes creates stress-induced illness or discomfort in any or all of the bodies (physical, mental, emotional).

Dominion — A higher order of angels commissioned to administer the will of God/Essence of ALL that IS.

ego — The personality self that when disciplined brings balance to the physical, mental and emotional bodies. When unbalanced, the ego displays controlling, selfish qualities. These qualities are broken down and transformed into compassion and loving detachment as lessons are learned toward soul integration.

Key Concepts

emotional body — That aspect of the lower-self triad (see right), which is housed in the solar plexus. The drama and turmoil of this body can be stilled by breaking emotional cycles and patterns, which balances the ego. Energy 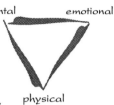 follows thought; thus, how we think affects the state of the emotional body. *See mental body and physical body.*

energy — The vibration and frequency of invisible molecules of Essence coursing through all aspects of who we are, what we are, making up where we are; the unseen expression of ALL that we are connected to ALL that IS.

enlightenment — A state of mind filtered through the heart center, electrifying the entire sense of being and acknowledging a supreme knowing and wisdom.

evolution of the soul — The unfolding process toward a higher level of knowing and consciousness individually; the awakening of the human form to the reality of Universal Oneness through the plan of love, light, truth and power.

glamour — A distortion of perception induced by the desires of the emotional body, thus encouraging the ego's need to control and manipulate. In the unfolding process of life's lessons, we dissipate our glamours and detach from the grip of the ego-based personality.

grace — The spiritual showering of higher energies from the Essence of All/God when a conscious shift has been made in one's level of knowingness and awareness. Grace is bestowed upon all who embrace the Essence of Nature and the Godness in it ALL.

Key Concepts

higher self — The wise aspect of the higher-self triad (see right), which guides you from the depths of your inner knowing when you listen with inner ears. See *intuition* and *will of the soul.*

will of the soul

higher self   intuition

I AM — Our identity with the presence of Spirit and Godhead; the indwelling union of "I and the Universe are one;" the affirmation of "I AM all that I AM in ALL that I AM;" we are this essence of all that is connected with the Essence of ALL that is.

illumination — An insight based on self-realization, which lights the path for greater clarity; one is illumined by a higher knowingness.

illusions — Falsehoods of reality, typically dressed up as truth to trick the self as to what is and what isn't. Oftentimes, an illusion is a mask to our greater good perpetuated by a group of people with the same thoughtform, thus the statement "hypnotic state of the world."

inner guidance — The gentle, still voice within always guiding your hand and lighting your path. Silence and stillness contribute to your ability to listen within; stress and drama inhibit your ability to feel your inner guidance.

intuition — An aspect of the higher-self triad, directing a higher level of consciousness beyond the rational mind. See *higher self* and *will of the soul.*

Key Concepts

mental body — That aspect of the lower-self triad that retains thought. The thought evolves as the mental body deconditions and expands its awareness of the individual. In the process, illusions melt away and clarity sets in. See *physical body* and *emotional body*.

neutrality — The bridge with which the midpoint of opposites formulates a sense of balance, unity, freedom, and unification.

physical body — That aspect of the lower-self triad pertaining to physical matter, through which the heart and soul are expressed. When ego/personality is unbalanced, the physical body displays symptoms of pain and tension. See *mental body* and *emotional body*.

right thinking — Thought can be constructive or destructive, creative or controlling; right thinking is about embracing the power of thought and directing it for right motion with right understanding of its subtle process.

soul — The essence of the higher-self triad (see diagram on page 102) that merges with the personality to form a balanced, whole sense of self. The soul is the interface between personality and Spirit; it expands the conscious level of being within the realm of all possibilities.

Spirit — Meaning "breath," the Universal breath of all of life; the Essence of nature's cosmic energetic connection; the breath of Universal Essence.

spiritual — The soul's evolution through lessons learned along the path. To be spiritual is to be your true essence and allow your goodness and greatness to be all that it is within you connected to the Source of your being, Universal Essence.

unconditional love — To love all parts of the whole, releasing all conditions and attachments to any fragment that makes up the whole; based on acceptance and truth in the present moment.

unfoldment — A Divine rightness of evolvement; through patience, trust and stillness, you experience an all-knowing, inner reality gently guiding you on your path.

universality — Embracing the quality of equality, openness, freedom and the core of Oneness; to be receptive to the realm of all natures of being.

veil — A tool of the ego created by the mental body to cloud the reality of what truly is and keep the self from furthering its full concept of self; used to distract the expansion of consciousness by masquerading as reality though it is an illusion.

wholeness — The synthesis and integration of the mental, emotional and physical bodies into a balanced, unified and healthy personality. In this recognized state, the soul (higher-self triad) can fuse with the balanced personality (lower-self triad). Thus, the Essence of ALL can guide the whole, synthesized person.

will of the soul — The aspect of the higher-self triad directed by the will/power principle of Universal Truth. See *higher self* and *intuition*.

Guided Meditation

Excerpted from the audiotape*
"View from the Mountaintop:
A Journey to Self-Renewal"

This is your time to relax. Know that your only point of power is in the present moment. This is the moment for you to allow yourself to let go and simply be. Just be. Give yourself permission to unlearn all the thoughts you have learned. Free your mind, free your thoughts, let go of any judgments. Feel freer and lighter as you situate yourself in a comfortable position. If you are in a chair, plant your feet firmly on the floor. If you are lying down, allow your arms and legs to be free from constriction. Get ready now for your personal journey into self-discovery and self-renewal.

As you **close your eyes,** focus your attention on your breathing. **Slowly inhale through your nose and slowly exhale through your mouth.** Breathe in peace, fulfillment, and confidence. Breathe out anxiety, tension and any limiting thoughts. Feel the supporting environment gently accept your body, as you slowly and gently sink into it. Begin to feel the peacefulness around you. Just relax, release, and let go.

Now scan your body from your head to your toes. Focus on the top of your head and **feel the relaxation flow through your entire being ... slowly.** Allow your face to go limp, release your jaw, sense the massaging effect of relaxation move through your scalp. A comfortable heaviness settles in your neck, radiating into the shoulders. Feel the warmth of relaxation penetrate down your arms, into your fingers and thumbs. As the wave of relaxation lingers, it begins to travel from the top of your spine to your hips. Your pelvis sinks deeper into the supporting environment as the flow of relaxation moves down your thighs, into your knees, releasing the lower legs and sending the relaxation out the bottom of your feet.

Be completely and totally immersed in the gentle relaxation. Allow yourself to be consumed by the soothing effect of muscular release. If you detect residual tension, focus on it, visualize, feel, and sense the warmth radiating into that area. The relaxation blends in harmony with the rest of the body. The total sum of the parts is now one, one whole mind, body, and spirit, relaxed and receptive to your inner love, truth and goodness.

Visualize yourself at the base of a beautiful, majestic mountain. Notice the surrounding environment; allow yourself to be one with the elements. Breathe deep the fresh mountain air; allow it to purify you. Feel a sense of security and safety where you are. Feel confident and competent. Own this place within you as a source of strength and encouragement. View the heavens above and feel the earth below as you joyfully anticipate your journey ahead.

Step back and examine the mountain. Gaze at the mountain's top and **observe the pathway below, carved by footprints in eight steps** representing your journey to self-renewal. The lengthy climb between each step provides opportunity to experience your essence. Venture toward the path now, leading up the base of the mountain.

Take your **first step to RELEASE.** Release from your life what no longer serves a purpose. Let go of self-imposed limitations that have been holding you back from your true potential. Begin now by accepting your goodness and releasing the doubts and fears of the past. **Say to yourself,** "I NOW WILLINGLY EMBRACE AND LOVE LIFE."

Your **second step is to AFFIRM & APPRECIATE.** Affirm your goodness and appreciate yourself for who and what you are in this present moment. Love yourself unconditionally for all the goodness you bring to the world. Your uniqueness is a gift. Appreciate and cherish it. You are a good person. **Say to yourself,** "I APPRECIATE MYSELF AND AFFIRM ALL THE GOODNESS IN MY LIFE."

The climb is steep to the **third step of CLARITY, PURPOSE & CLEAR INTENTION.** Create the vision of your dreams. Be clear. Clarity aligns your physical, mental, emotional and spiritual self. When you ask for clarity, get silent, and go within. **Say to yourself,** "I SEEK AND FIND CLARITY AND PURPOSE IN MY LIFE."

Striving toward the mountain's summit, step up to the **fourth step to achieve BALANCE.** All change can bring balance and peace in your life when viewed in clear thought. How you respond to the world around you creates your inner balance. It is the midpoint of opposites; it is achieving neutrality; it is moderation. **Say to yourself,** "I AM LIVING A LIFE IN BALANCE AND STABILITY."

You're feeling very strong now as you step up to the **fifth step of LIGHTHEARTEDNESS.** Simply let go of the boundaries, explore the unknown, learn to laugh and really feel it. When you laugh, you free your heart of any heaviness; feel it getting lighter. Give yourself permission to free your inhibitions, get silly and let your inner child out to play. **Say to yourself,** "I AM FILLED WITH THE LOVING ENERGY OF LIGHTHEARTEDNESS."

As you venture forward, feel your entire mind, body and spirit pull you up to the **sixth step of LOVE.** Love is the foundation of life, it is the wisdom of the heart. Your love sustains and heals you. **Say to yourself,** "I AM FILLED WITH THE ESSENCE OF LOVE. THE MORE LOVE I SEND OUT, THE MORE LOVE I RECEIVE. I LOVE MYSELF UNCONDITIONALLY."

Feel your essence emerging as you lift yourself up to the **seventh step—RECEIVE.** Receive all the gifts and blessings that are yours. Listen in your heart and spirit; know you are worthy to receive. Open yourself to receive your abundance NOW. **Say to yourself,** "I WILLINGLY RECEIVE ALL THE GOODNESS THAT IS MINE."

You meet your eighth and final step on your journey, the **step to THANKFULNESS.** To perpetuate your goodness, always be grateful for the changes in your life. Give thanks to your higher power for the abundance that is yours. **Say to yourself,** "I AM THANKFUL TO MY HIGHER POWER FOR THE ABUNDANCE THAT IS MINE."

As you rise to the summit of the mountain, you are filled with elation, self-acceptance and self-respect. **Feel**

the beauty surrounding you and within you. Embrace the partnership of your mind, body and spirit—the oneness, the wholeness, the ability to flow freely within yourself. You are your essence.

Recognize your inner strength and beauty. You are filled with courage, wisdom, truth, and inner peace. **Feel lighter, freer, unencumbered.** This sense of lightness lifts you above the endless ebb and flow of life. You now acquire a broader vision; you see the goodness in everyone. You develop clear intention, purpose, and manifest goals. Your knowingness is magnified. **Feel the sense of self-renewal.** This is yours.

You feel accomplished, confident, and competent. Your heart is affirmed by your goodness. Your heart is knowing. Your heart is filled with laughter. Your heart is willing to give and receive. Just sit back and view your journey with a sense of awe and appreciation. Keep your feet firm in the earth, as your mind, heart, and spirit remain in the heavens. Stretch yourself. **Believe in yourself.** Hold on to your truth.

Continue to fill yourself with the riches of Essence and the richness of Grace. **Be filled with all that empowers your mind, body and spirit** as you review the eight steps:

1 — Release
2 — Affirm and Appreciate
3 — Discover Purpose and Clear Intention
4 — Achieve Balance
5 — Embrace Lightheartedness
6 — Love
7 — Receive
8 — Give Thanks

Feel a sense of invigoration and self-renewal, and know each and every day you are getting better and better.

Now bring your awareness and your consciousness back into this place and space. Take your time and breathe deep a complete inhalation, feel the revitalization and invigoration, and slowly exhale. Inhale deeply and completely and stretch your arms up overhead as if it's your first big yawn of the day and slowly and completely exhale.

Know that you can take yourself to the mountain's summit at any time during your day and experience your journey of self-renewal. Simply close your eyes and visualize yourself on your mountaintop. You are at peace with yourself and all around you, and in silence you **say to yourself,** "I AM THE LIGHT OF MY TRUTH. I AM ... ."

As you become familiar with the meditation, let yourself relax and simply focus on the words in **bold print** to guide you. With practice, you may eventually find you only need to glance at the list of steps. Use whatever works for you to journey into this relaxation, meditation, and contemplation time.

*To order a complete copy of the audiotape "View from the Mountaintop: A Journey to Self-Renewal," refer to the order form in the back of this book.

About
the Author

Lee Ann Fagan Dzelzkalns is married and the mother of two wonderful boys. She specializes in a heart-centered approach to facilitating and teaching about the nature of being whole (in body, mind, emotions, heart, soul and spirit). The natural healing quality of her work is transformative; it focuses on self-acceptance, self-honor, self-love, self-empowerment and self-realization.

She has experience as a medical social worker, with a master's degree in exercise and sports science. With an extensive background in relaxation, guided-imagery work, and years of study and commitment on her own spiritual path, Lee Ann gently guides others to experience the potential and rhythm of wholeness in their lives.

Lee Ann resides with her family in Whitefish Bay, Wisconsin.

The Nature of Being Whole®
Products

Selected poems and illustrations in this book are available in inspirational cards. For information on these and other products available through Ageless Dominion Publishing, contact us at:

P.O. Box 11546
Milwaukee, WI 53211
(414) 332-6775

Please use the order form below to order additional copies of "View from the Mountaintop: A Journey Into Wholeness."

Also available through
Ageless Dominion Publishing:

View from the Mountaintop:
A Journey to Self-Renewal

A Guided Meditation Tape

"... a superb relaxation tape utilizing visualization techniques made all the more potent by the sincerity of Lee Ann's voice ... angelic piano harmonies are in perfect sync with her glorious message."   —Richard Fuller
Metaphysical Reviews